10/12 W9-AVO-177

WITHDRAWN

FURRY HAMSTERS/
HÁMSTERES PELUDOS

By Katie Kawa   Traducción al español: Eduardo Alamán

Gareth Stevens
Publishing

Please visit our website, www.garethstevens.com. For a free color catalog of all our high-quality books, call toll free 1-800-542-2595 or fax 1-877-542-2596.

Library of Congress Cataloging-in-Publication Data

Kawa, Katie.
  [Furry hamsters. Spanish & English]
  Furry hamsters = Hámsteres peludos / Katie Kawa.
      p. cm. — (Pet corner = Rincón de las mascotas)
  Includes index.
  ISBN 978-1-4339-5607-2 (library binding)
  1. Hamsters as pets—Juvenile literature. I. Title. II. Title: Hámsteres peludos.
  SF459.H3K3918 2011
  636.935'6—dc22

                              2011004294

First Edition

Published in 2012 by
Gareth Stevens Publishing
111 East 14th Street, Suite 349
New York, NY 10003

Editor: Katie Kawa
Designer: Andrea Davison-Bartolotta
Spanish Translation: Eduardo Alamán

Photo credits: Cover, pp. 1, 5, 7, 15, 17, 21, 23, 24 (paws) Shutterstock.com; pp. 9, 11, 13, 24 (cage, pellets) iStockphoto.com; p. 19 iStockphoto/Thinkstock.

Printed in the United States of America

CPSIA compliance information: Batch #CS11GS: For further information contact Gareth Stevens, New York, New York at 1-800-542-2595.

Contents

Contenido

Hamsters love to play!

¡Los hámsteres son muy juguetones!

A hamster runs to stay healthy. It runs in a wheel.

Los hámsteres corren para mantenerse sanos. Este hámster corre en una rueda.

Hamsters run inside balls. This keeps them from getting lost.

Los hámsteres corren dentro de esferas. Así no se pierden.

A hamster lives in a cage. The cage is cleaned every week.

Los hámsteres viven en jaulas. Las jaulas se limpian cada semana.

Hamsters eat special food. These are called pellets.

Los hámsteres comen granos, semillas, nueces y una comida seca llamada "pellets."

Hamsters eat fruits and vegetables too.

Los hámsteres también comen frutas y verduras.

Hamsters have pouches in their cheeks. This is where they keep food.

Los hámsteres tienen bolsitas en sus mejillas. En estas bolsas guardan su comida.

A hamster chews its toys. This keeps its teeth short.

Los hámsteres mordisquean sus juguetes. Así mantienen sus dientes cortos.

A hamster cleans itself. It licks its paws and wipes its fur.

Los hámsteres se limpian solos. Los hámsteres se lamen las patas y el pelaje.

21

Hamsters have soft fur.
They like when people
pet them.

Los hámsteres tienen
pelaje suave. A los
hámsteres les gusta
que los acaricien.

Words to Know/ Palabras que debes saber

paws/
(las) patas

pellets/
(las) bolitas

pouches/
(las) bolsas

Index / Índice